THE QUEEN OF INGLEWOOD

The Queen of Inglewood

By Teka Lark

Word Palace Press
P.O. Box 583
San Luis Obispo, CA 93406
wordpalacepress.com
wordpalacepress@aol.com

Book Cover and Layout Design
Garrett Stotko

Author Photograph
Kate Albright

Book Typeset In
NiteClub
Linux Libertine

ISBN: 0-9754653-3-3
ISBN-13: 978-0-9754653-3-2

The Following Poems Have Been Previously Published in Other Works:

"Random Violence"
(The Coiled Serpent: Poets Arising from the Cultural Quakes and Shifts of Los Angeles);

"Fine Art" and *"#DTLA is not Racist"*
(Angel City Review);

"Party Monster"
(Writ Large Press).

For my grandmothers Izora and Lily and
Professor Mark (Buddy) Roberts

Prelude

In 1939 the Academy Theater was built in Inglewood by Charles Lee. The purpose was to hold the Oscars, but it was not to be. Inglewood is the B actress that never quite made it. Inglewood is my hometown.

Are you ready for your close up? Smile. You're beautiful. You don't look a day over 29.

This time you're going to make it.

Cast of Characters

The Holly Golightly Suite

gin and tonic, makes it all go away-larkism

In Arcadia off of El Camino and Tenth

They say it is going to rain.

They say it's going to rain harder than it ever has, so I can't go outside, because if it rains, then I'll get wet and if I get wet, then I could catch a cold and if I catch a cold I could get pneumonia, and if I got pneumonia I could possibly die.

I have to stay at home, because they say that it is going to rain.

In Tulip, Texas there was this twister and it destroyed people's homes and it took people and tossed them in the air and being tossed through the air, that can't be good, can it?

In Los Angeles when it rains there are lots of accidents, lots of people not paying attention and sliding all over the place, driving their cars like they aren't pieces of two ton death traps made out of metal that can crush a baby's head, the way a snail is crushed when you accidentally step on him,
because he is in your way.

Cars are very dangerous and when it rains they are even more dangerous.
Cars and rain together, you might as well just get it over with and kill yourself with Diazepam, because at least that won't hurt as much and you won't risk something, like actually living through the accident, how horrible would that be,
I had a friend once, he had to get physical therapy,
it seemed quite difficult.

This is why I have to stay home, because they say it is going to rain.

I was going to be this actor when I came out from Texas, but I didn't know how to act, because out here you have to act all of the time.

In Arcadia off of El Camino and Tenth

(Continued)

I had this audition, it was for a big movie, a role in this movie by that
famous director, but on the day of the audition it rained,
so I couldn't go, I think it was a good decision, because what if I had died.

I can't go outside when it's raining.

Paul Varjack

You know my son, he really is great, he's a straight A student,
he's a quarterback on the football team, and he's a "good boy", if
you know what I mean,
No fooling around for him.

He is such a happy boy with a promising future, because he's
got drive and ambition, he knows what's truly important, and he
stays away from the girls, because they are nothing but trouble
anyway.

No he doesn't fool with the girls; he just studies, exercises, reads
the Bible, and goes to bed.

My son he is such a good boy, he is going to Stanford, you know
that is a top school, we worked really hard for this.

I decided that he needed to be around the right kind of people,
because if a boy is going to have a future he's got to be surround-
ed by other people who are going to have a future, and he is such
a good boy.

My son, he takes after me, he got his brains from me, because
I was a good student, I could have went to college, but I had to
work while Lee was in school and then the baby came and then
the other baby came, and so here I am, but I'm really happy, because look at my son, so good, so smart, so full of promise.

My beautiful son, we have big plans, everything we worked for
has been for this moment.

My son is a really good boy.

Breakfast at Kate Mantilini

Sharon's dog got hit by a car, I saw it, but I didn't tell her. Everyday
dogs die and no one really cares, so why should I tell
Sharon about her dog?

I saw it happen and I saw the car too.
It was a big tan Mercedes, with tinted windows, and the driver was
on their mobile phone.

Sharon's poor little dog, didn't even have a chance.

When the big tan Mercedes hit him, the driver didn't stop the car or
even slow it down,
but it did fly a little,
because of the impact.

Then her dog wasn't a dog anymore, but road kill;
trash in the middle
of the street.

It was sort of her fault anyway, if she had let him go outside
sometimes, this would have never happened.

A dog, a big one can't just hang out in the house all day.

So I thought, better Sharon think that he ran away,
than to know that he became
pieces of smashed, bloody, trash on the street.

I suspect Sharon knows what happened anyway.

Fran Kubelik Has a Nice Apartment

I have begun placing fake food in my refrigerator in order to not have to waste five minutes of my life answering annoying questions.

"You only have vodka in your refrigerator, don't you shop?"

People are always asking you questions that they don't actually care to know the answer to, they simply want to be nosy and prying.

So I have begun to put fake food in my refrigerator and my cabinets, I used to put fake canned goods in my refrigerator, but then I had smart asses telling me that I could get botulism if I did that and that was a longer conversation than the fridge filled with vodka conversation.

"Do you know if you put leave canned goods in the refrigerator that you could get botulism?"

No I didn't, thanks for your concern, oh and I also didn't know that smoking could give me cancer or that driving while drunk could get me arrested, and that mosquitoes can kill me, thanks so much for your advice, I truly appreciate that.

I'm going to buy some bug spray right now.

So now I put fake fresh vegetables in my refrigerator and I now remember to put the fake canned goods in my cabinets, to cut off people who seem to be a wealth of useless information.

I bought them at the toy store, they are shockingly realistic, like the guns the toy stores used to sell, and in plastic, they look like legitimate food.

Fran Kubelik Has a Nice Apartment

(Continued)

I have also begun to put up fake pictures, for years I never had pictures of anyone in my apartment, but now that I have begun to have visitors, and people want to know where's my mom and dad sort of like when I was four and that woman came by my mom's motel room.

"She's at the store, we're on our way to visit my dad in California, she's coming back, she's a good mom, look I'm here reading this book and I'm only four also observe the clean and sparkliness of me, now go away you've done your job."

So now I have pictures of my mother and father, not my real mother and father, but people who would look like they could be my mother and father if Target was God and Ikea was a set designer.

I picked out the picture because of the mom, she was pretty and she had glasses and looked like someone that could maybe be my mother, my real mother looked nothing like me, but the woman in this picture even though she isn't real, is more like what I would want my mother to look like, more like how other people would want my mother to look like, and then instead of an odd stare people would just say "she's pretty, can I have some water," so I put her by my computer.

Now when people come over I'm prepared with my fake food in the refrigerator and my fake family on my computer stand, now I just need to add some cool things to my medicine cabinets.

A great apartment
it's all about the right accessories.

Party Monster

I found the hottest thing
Hotter than cocaine in 1988
Hotter than a 14 year old having sex with her mom's new boyfriend
Hotter than taking Dexedrine
and completing one hundred typed pages of nonsense on hour 52 of no
sleep
Hotter than a drunken orgy with your English professor, that brilliant
guy who snorted the blood out of your heart, and that almost underage
kid from the early entry program.

And it's easy, pretty easy
So easy it's like God wants you to do it
Like he wants you to have sex
And he wants you to smoke pot
And he wants you to boil coca leaves and drink them in a tea God wants
you to get addicted to hot stuff,
if he didn't he wouldn't have made the hot stuff so easy
And it's pretty easy and it's old school
Sodom and Gomorrah old school
It's Cain and Abel old school.

IT's Murder
It's the new hot thing.
Is it morbid?
Of course it is.
Is it thin?
It's hot, so it has to be.
Is it illegal?
Sure it is, but so is cocaine.
Is it vegan?
I'm not sure.
But murder is exciting and easy, pretty easy.

Party Monster

(Continued)

I remember the first time I murdered someone,
I met them at a library after taking massive amounts of amphetamines,
Then because of my charming personality
I invited them back to my place
And then when they sat down on my couch
And said the code word;
They didn't know it was the code word,
that wouldn't have been hot or any fun,
it would have been like having sex with someone who's kind of drunk, but
they insist on finishing
That's annoying and not so hot or easy.

So after they said the codeword
I offed them.

I felt,
"Oh man they're dead," but you know at the same time "Wow they're dead
and I did that."
It was such a feeling of accomplishment
Like when I convinced the doctor that I was ok (even though I wasn't)
and I got to go home
and hang out with this guy I saw a lot at that time
He was brilliant
He was into eye-gazing.

I extinguished a human life,
like I did when I put out that grease fire when I was a RA, cool.
I helped with population control,
that's a true need.
And I realized it was easy, pretty easy.

Most people don't really care if their neighbor never talks to them again or
if their mother stops calling them forever.
My mother stopped calling me, but I didn't kill her,

(Continued)

she killed herself,
but the phone calls did stop
I've murdered lots of mothers and fathers too
and a bunch of neighbors,
especially the ones with the loud barking dogs that always have the TV
up to the loudest volume
and with those people you get a sort of two for one,
because house pets need alive owners.

And most people are nice to loud neighbors, they're, usually pretty nice
they start off normally with a polite semi-anonymous note

*Could you quiet it down, while I know that your unemployment status has
made the computer your best friend, I have job, that I am trying to keep in
order to keep the cost of my prescriptions at a minimum, though I'm pretty
sure I could steal some from my 25 year old step-mother, but I want to be
independent, because I'm an adult and I'm responsible, I am a teacher, I
teach the future, so if you care about the future could you turn your best
friend down, just a little, I have headphones, you can borrow them?*

Usually that just makes them louder and encourages them to buy more
pets!

When you murder that person, you know, no one cares, everyone's
happy, no more loud pet sounds, no more faint chanting of reality TV or
the staged moanings of Internet porn coming
through the
thin walls.

It's almost as if it was as God intended, and it's easy, pretty easy,
like scoring drugs
or finding someone skanky to have sex with at a bar.

Party Monster

(Continued)

And it's therapeutic.
And it's so easy.

When you kill someone
it's like
you get a little piece
of their soul.
It's spiritual.
It's like the tantra.
It's pretty.

My best friend, who's easy and pretty,
I met her at the hospital
We keep in touch
Giving each other advice on how to appear ok

She doubted the sensation, but I showed her how to do it, because it's easy,
it's pretty easy and now she has murdered more people than me
AND
she's lost
ten more pounds.

All the more reason to participate,
you can never be too thin, now can you?
It's better than no carbs for your metabolism.

Her husband won't let her talk to me anymore,
He says I'm a bad influence
He thinks she's having an affair with me
I'm sure he doesn't know about the murdering thing
But I email her at her secret account

So you should try it, it's the new hot thing and it's easy, it's pretty easy.

The Daisy Buchanan Suite
(as played by mia farrow)

i have a fast metabolism-larkism

A Second on Candy

When you eat a piece of candy it makes you happy,
It is a two minute space of time,
Where you think,
"Yum good!"
But candy doesn't add anything,
It is just about the now,
It rots your teeth,
It spoils your dinner,
My husband sometimes says,
"You're like a piece of candy."

Fay Buchanan

When Fay goes out she puts on her sunglasses and always remembers to bring her pack of cigarettes.

In the bars you have to have props, not like a gun or a lamp, but more like figurative props.

A cool back story, "I was originally from Turkey, but my parents moved here when I was one or maybe it was two."
A cool front story, "I'm an actress, I've been in quite a few avant-garde films."
A humanizing element, "On the weekends I spend time with old people."

Tonight Fay has all of her stories memorized and she has her perfect jeans on, which makes her in her mind a triple threat.

Mysterious
Fascinating
A person that looks really good in jeans

Fay has perfected the art of airy conversation.

"I can't believe that really popular movie is liked by so many people, because it's really stupid, but most people are really stupid, it's a good thing that I'm not one of those really stupid people."

Fay is a graduate of a top college, she was also the graduate of a top high school, and her parents were graduates of top colleges and they were graduates of top high schools, so that means Fay is smart times two or is it four?

In casual conversation Fay always reminds people, "I'm the graduate of a top college and a top high school, but you know it's really no big deal."

Fay Buchanan

(Continued)

Fay always likes to bring up things that she thinks aren't big deals.

Fay smokes too much, because she gets nervous and it helps her not eat as much, she had to go to fat camp once, so she's a little paranoid about her weight.

But tonight is a good night, because she's a triple threat.

Mysterious
Fascinating
A person who looks really good in jeans

Fay wears her sunglasses even when it rains, because she thinks they make her look better.

An Object of Love

"That is the pill that makes me feel funny."

Violet's a seven year old drug addict, but it's ok because it's sanctioned by her parents and a MD.

Violet is loved.

Her mother spent $50,000 to bring Violet into the world.

Her mother lost five fetuses before she was blessed with Violet, she didn't want to adopt, because you never know what "kind" of a degenerate you might get if you adopt.

Violet was born via C-section, so that her mom could get a tummy tuck after, because she wanted to look her very best when Violet came into the world.

Violet's mother could fit into her size 4 jeans after she was born.

Violet is loved.

Her mother resigned from her job as a consultant when Violet was born, because she wanted to dedicate all of her time to Violet.

When Violet turned two her first words were to the woman who helped to take care of her, that made Violet's mom sad, so she signed up for extra yoga classes and asked her doctor for a prescription to help her sleep.

Violet used to like moving around a lot, she never sat down, so her mother took her to a specialist, who gave her pills.

Violet's been taking meds since she was four, because they help her mommy to love her.

Farrah Fawcett Seems Happy or don't worry about your soul, you can buy a new one at the dentist office

I woke up in the morning after a night of watching Charlie's Angel reruns and realized that I needed to get my teeth capped, all of them, not caps, but maybe porcelain veneers, I heard that those are more durable, but I realized that would cost more and my health insurance wasn't going to cover that. Farrah Fawcett worked on TV, so she didn't have to worry about such things

A fabulous grin will get you places.
During the day I kept thinking about ways that I could make money so that I could get a fabulous grin, a movie star one, a friend told me once that movie star's teeth look fake, which may be true, but it never seems to stop people from going to the movies. Farrah Fawcett had range she did Burning Bed.

A fabulous grin will take you far.

People say that my teeth look great, I had braces for seven years, so I guess they should look great, but I feel that they could look a little better, a little brighter, a little more perfect, your teeth are your windows to opportunities, and big, bright, white ones, think about how many opportunities those could bring about. Farrah Fawcett was from Texas and she made it all the way to Los Angeles, and ended up being an actress, a famous one.

A fabulous grin will give your face a new fresh look.

The thing about porcelain veneers is that they have to shave your real teeth down in order to place the veneers on, which means that you wouldn't have teeth anymore, the roots would be there, but the enamel would be gone, but it's a finality kind of cosmetic procedure, meaning it's something you would have to keep up forever, and your real teeth if you take care of them are suppose to last forever, but I don't think I have done such a good job taking care of my teeth. Farrah Fawcett set records in poster sales simply because you could see her nipples, in the 70s I guess that was a big deal.

(Continued)

A fabulous grin will impress co-workers and assist you in making new interesting friends.

In the LA Weekly I saw an ad for veneers for a discounted price, but discounted cosmetic procedures have never seemed like a good idea, being beautiful shouldn't be cheap, it should cost money, because if it didn't everyone could be beautiful and what would be the point of being beautiful if it didn't mean that you were more beautiful than everyone else. Everyone copied Farrah's flip, but it didn't look quite the same on chubby girls from the middle of the country.

A fabulous grin can open doors to new opportunities.

And if I got veneers, could I still smoke? Would that stain my veneers, if I somehow made enough money in some kind of a devious plot to get whiter teeth would smoking still be an option, would I have to stop, would I gain ten pounds thus losing all of the friends I had attained with my new porcelain perfect teeth. I think Farrah Fawcett uses a lot of drugs, but she says she's doesn't, and why would she lie?

A fabulous grin will make you more confident.

Better teeth would make me feel better about myself, I would not need to worry about friends, though I would have them, because of my great teeth, but I wouldn't care about things like my jeans or my make-up or my manicure, because I would be completely confident in my new perfect grin.

I will go get some beautiful fake teeth tomorrow, I'll just charge them, I shouldn't do it, but brand new teeth will make the inside of me feel so much better, so it's worth it, I'm worth it.

Do you think Farrah's teeth are real?
Me neither.

My Best Fiend

Do you want to be my very best friend?
I think we should be.
I think we should be very best friends.
We can call each other every day.
We can share intimate secrets.
I can introduce you as:
        This is (put your name here) and she's my very best friend.
We could act inappropriately close.
Then people would whisper things like, "I think they are a little too close,
you know what I mean," wink wink.
And then we could get very drunk at parties and make out,
that would freak everyone out.
That would be fun.
So do you want to be my
Best Friend.

Jane Burden

Jane doesn't eat meat, because it can kill you,
Jane doesn't talk to people, because they are annoying,
Jane doesn't open herself up, because she could potentially get hurt,
Jane is a revolutionary.
Jane got her heart broken once, by her mother, "You look a little chunky
Jane, you really need to watch it, you used to be so cute."
Jane sleeps around a lot, but Jane doesn't feel anything, because she
is a revolutionary. Jane doesn't wear leather shoes, Jane doesn't shop
at corporate supermarkets, Jane doesn't eat dairy, Jane doesn't believe
in marriage, Jane doesn't believe in procreation, Jane doesn't believe
in cell phones, because the only people who call are people who don't
really care about you anyway, Jane doesn't believe in religion, because
it's a tool to oppress the masses. Jane doesn't watch movies that aren't
subtitled, unless of course they are British, Jane doesn't watch broadcast
television, Jane doesn't eat at chain Chinese restaurants, because she
only likes bringing home–
authentic take-out.
Jane doesn't use plastic to carry her groceries in.
Jane doesn't patronize museums that exhibit pieces produced mainly by
men.
Jane doesn't sugar coat her true emotions.
Jane doesn't shy away from being mean to stupid people.
Jane doesn't shy away from a confrontation, because she feels that her
open-mindedness to trying new things and her vastness of human experience as well as her ability to experience empathy turns confrontations
into more of her sharing her opinions with those who are lesser than.
Jane doesn't date people who drive SUVs.
Jane doesn't date people who haven't lived outside the country, because
if you haven't truly experienced another culture then how could she
possibly talk to you. Jane doesn't date people who aren't dedicating
their life to a cause bigger than themselves.
Jane doesn't date people who don't treat her with anything less than.
Jane doesn't date much.

Jane Burden

(Continued)

Jane doesn't listen to people much.
Jane doesn't have many girlfriends, because she finds most women really dumb.
Jane has spent a lifetime not doing anything,
because she cares about others.
Jane doesn't believe in anything, because Jane is, a revolutionary.

Go Ask Alice Suite

everyone loves Hello Kitty!!!!-larkism

Le divorce de Théophile Gautier

In ballet they won't allow you to do Pointe Work if you are fat, because Pointe Work is to make the dancer "appear" weightless and being fat would completely make this technique pointless.

American women, who have the bodies of little girls, dancing on the tips of their toes, moving gracefully to moves with French names, and music by Italian and German composers.

"Jete battu!!! Again. Jete battu !!!Again. Jete battu!!!" Again. Yells the dance instructor in her Russian accented English and French, and actually dance instructor says she's not Russian, but Ukrainian.

A 38 year old former ballerina that looks 58, because of the diet of cigarettes and coffee that she's kept since she was 14 to keep her svelte figure, she used to be with the Bolshoi, "You are lazy, all lazy, and you, silly girl with the blue ribbon, you need to practice more you look like an ox...lazy Americans!!!"

Dance instructor's career was cut short by another ballerina, yes another ballerina, a better one, a younger one, a healthier one, a more pleasant one, with strong legs, with good feet, and now dance instructor is here, in America, teaching young women with little girl bodies the art of ballet.

A life dedicated to the dance.

A life dedicated to practice, practice, and more practice. A life that's dedication has made her the proud owner of feet that will never look pretty in sandals, because Pointe Work if you don't have good feet, takes your feet and makes them into stumps with black toenails, if you are lucky, and if you are not lucky, stumps with no toenails at all. A life that's made her the owner of legs that other women envy, but will never be naked in the light, pronounced striations on a tool, that's softness has been practiced away to produce the perfect arabesque, look grotesque without the correct lighting and the mask of tights.

(Continued)

A life dedicated to the performance. A life dedicated to the perfection of art. A life dedicated to the perfection of perfection.

No ice cream sodas or even an occasional cookie without thinking about the location of the bathroom, the location of the Ipecac, the location of people's eyes, because if you don't think, if you don't practice, if you don't stay under control you never know where the things that go in, could potentially end up sticking out.

Bad teeth and brittle bones are a small price to pay to be perfect, to be the best, even if it's only for a petite allegro.

The Bolshoi threw dance instructor away, so now she teaches other dancers who want to be ballerinas, the art of appearing weightless.

Mr. DD Bagley's Daughter's Recipe for French Fries.

This is how you make French Fries.

Take a pan, a potato, a bottle of oil, and a bottle of gin, for taste, cut up the potato and place it on the pan.

Arrange the cut up fries in a way that will look appetizing to guest, in case after they are finished cooking you don't have time to place them in a fashionable serving tray.

Take the bottle of oil and pour it over the French Fries.

Oh and remember to preheat your oven to 300 or 400 degrees, no need to get anal about it, because you aren't going to eat the fries anyway, this is all pretend, but in a real way, because there is a point to this, eating the fries isn't the point though.

Ok now place the pan with the attractively arranged julienned potatoes covered with oil into the oven, in about ten minutes or when you smell smoke, whatever comes first, take yourself out of the house.

While you're outside tell the responsible person that you hang out with when your fun associates are predisposed that you already called the police, but don't actually call them, because if you do that what you are trying to do won't get done.

Now when the house burns down make sure to look very tense, like you feel badly about the scene that has just transpired, but don't feel bad in a real way, because the point of this is not to feel bad, but to have fun, and to make French Fries.

Then tell the person who thinks you are her friend that you feel super bad about her house and then go to your boyfriend's house, well not your boyfriend, just some guy you see when you get bored, but you get bored a lot, so you see him a lot.

(Continued)

Don't worry about your parent's, because you were making French Fries and they, they being your parents are open-minded and reasonable people, they've read all the proper books written by other open-minded reasonable people with lots of abbreviations behind their name and because of that they have spent lots of quality time, with you, not lots of time, but quality, which is better, so they know and believe you truly must have been making French Fries and something just went horribly wrong, while making the French Fries, and it couldn't have been intentional, at least not the other part.

And that is how you make French Fries at home, because McDonald doesn't take American Express and no matter what they say a guy always appreciates a girl who can

whip up a meal with fourteen years notice.

Rick James Made Me Do It

Cocaine is a hell of a drug.

At least that's what Rick James said.
Fond memories of me and Brooke and Jen in the bathroom of a school
absent of boys so we couldn't sin, doing lines before Trig.

Cocaine is a hell of drug.

The sins of the rock star are visited upon the children, oh my.
I empathize with that Haidl kid and that girl he raped, because I was at
that party.

Listening to Superfreak.

That's what probably gave us the idea, you know that it was ok, I was
sitting at the edge having my spaced invaded by some other 15 year old
with a mouth, holding a cigarette, with my mind sort of gyrating from
topic to topic, because of something that someone's older sibling gave me,
and I saw that girl.

I saw her, I saw one kid from a good family after another, go forward
and back behind the pretty tan legs with the Jimmyz skirt beside it, but I
thought she was laughing, and I think I was laughing too, and we were all
cheering for her, you know she had told me the day before in AP Chem
that she wanted to be a porn star, but with a purpose I guess like that girl
from USC, Annabel Chong from the "I can't believe I did the whole team"
fame, you know she's from a good family too, I wonder who her favorite
musician is?

Cocaine is a hell of a drug.

Many people didn't appreciate Rick James and his value to society.
They would say things like he's a corrupting force with no class and plat-
forms and freaky braids and freak songs with dirty double meanings

(Continued)

like 69 times, love gun, and 17.
Lots of people from the 70s did not appreciate the nastiness that was created in the 80s.
My mother didn't.

She wouldn't allow me to listen to Rick James in her car.
"Why mom, why can't I listen to Rick James."
"You can't listen to it in my car, because it's oppressive to women." As long as you don't hear it, I guess the song never happened.
I guess that is why she never saw any of dad's songs, she was a smart woman, she had a PhD, what a smarty.

What do parents know, cocaine is a hell of a drug, Rick James knew what was truly going on, drugs complete the circle of life, why take Prozac when you can just do coke, it's like Ritalin for those who have hit puberty, if society can understand why eight year olds need their meds to get through the third grade, then people should understand that an adult needs their drug of choice to get through their third decade.

In school it helped me get all A's, it helped me stay awake to do all of those tests, and go to all of those parties, it helped me be ok with getting all B's and then C's, and it helped me when I got sent away to that "special" school.

"How does a twelve year old from a good family with hippie values become a dead twenty three year old on Sunset, I thought he just smoked a little pot?"

When things got bad I would think, hmmm
What would Mary Jane do?
She would let you inhale her and pass her around and around and around.
Of course you can't take her home to mother, but she is all right, yes she is all right, the girl's all right, yeeaaaah.

Rick James Made Me Do It

(Continued)

Rick James turned me into a social deviant.

Cocaine is a hell of a drug, but I used a good lapsed Catholic's soccer mom's husband bank account to pay for it.

Old Girl From Evergreen

She got tripped everyday in the hall, but we honestly didn't see her.

She didn't stand out,
but yet managed to be odd.

"Carrie's someone's sitting there,"

Who did she think she was, we didn't even know her.

And I think she was sleeping with her brother or was it her sister or was
it her dog or maybe it was that freak she hung out, I can't remember,
I just remember something odd about her.

Then she ran for prom queen,
if she thought that kind of thing was silly, you know
dressing like someone who wasn't homeless, the jocks,
the cheerleaders,
then what did she want our vote for.

Why would she think we would let her in?

After she spent four years
telling us
how wrong
we were.

What did she think would happen?

So we played a little trick.

The she gets all psychotic and uses her telepathic powers to try to kill us.

Old Girl From Evergreen

(Continued)

I wondered for a second,
why the sad face,
until the co-captain of the cheerleading squad's head exploded,

she was my best friend,

at least that week she was.

She should have been happy,
at least she was right,
so it should have been satisfying,
I like being right.

What a sore loser,
but she did say sports were barbaric.

You know I saw her at our tenth year reunion, she's in HR now,
and she's was still mad about that little incident.

So maybe us tripping her everyday and dropping pigs blood on her head
wasn't such a bad idea.

What a bitter weirdo.

But honestly we didn't see her,
we weren't mean,
if we had saw her,
that would have been mean,
and we aren't mean.

You Can't Ask Alice, because She's Dead

Hello Kitty is so cute,
But she doesn't have a mouth.
She has lots of outfits and lots of friends,
one even gave her wings,
but she's got no hole,
In her face.
She can't say ouch or stop or use the safeword.
But she is the best kitty,
People don't buy your accessories,
If you aren't a good kitty.
Everyone always think that Hello Kitty's smiling,
Because she is so cute.
But Hello Kitty is never smiling,
Because she doesn't have a mouth.

Norma Desmond Suite

taste like candy, feel like vicodin-larkism

The Senior Class President's Antagonist

Margaret polishes everyday with lemon pledge.

She polishes her table, her chairs, her windows, her mirrors, her kids, and her cats.

She has to make sure everything is clean, because you never know when someone might come by for a visit.

She checks frantically every hour on the hour for dust, for dirt, for a spot that is not shiny.

Her friends stopped calling, sick of the smell.
Her kids hate her, sick of the cleaning.
Her husband moved away, sick of living with a neurotic.

Margaret was a child protégé, valedictorian of her high school class, graduated from college at twenty, and went on to get a PhD, which she received at 23, but she was never quite happy, she felt she was suppose to get a little bit more, she was a PhD, a child protégé, a genius.

At 27 she fell off the track, she tried to get back on, but at 33 she realized that it was too late.

At first she only polished weekly, but then she had a visitor, a 21 year old visitor, who said, "I like your table, but it's slightly dusty," a flippant comment, but Margaret took this quite personally and she thought

"Oh no, I'm dirty, and people notice!!!!"

After that Margaret began to polish with more frequency, every visit to the grocery store included a visit to the cleaning aisle where she bought more lemon pledge, her weekly cleanings became biweekly and moved on to tri-weekly, but every week her visitors would get younger and younger and younger and they always had to say something,

The Senior Class President's Antagonist

(Continued)

"Let me take this dish to the sink,"
"That table is so vintage,"
"This looks like the chair I bought at Ikea," so she began to polish every
day attempting to preemptively strike any potential comments about her
lack of cleanliness.

Margaret slowly was unable to accept any more visitors, because she had
to polish.

So every day Margaret polishes with lemon pledge,
so if by chance she has visitors

they will know that her house,
is the cleanest on the block.

Ready for My Replay

Desmond wore his letterman jacket every day as he went to work,
He wore it to keep warm,
While he was loading the trucks,
He had been the star running,
Back on the Uni High School football team, circa 1988,
He was going to get a scholarship,
But then he got hurt,
Desmond works the swing shift,
Part time.
It's ok, because he never has to get up too early and when he's off he can go to the local
10086 bar,
To reminisce,
Last week he saw his old Uni Football team on the local news,
Desmond's rushing record had been broken,

"I was better than that guy Joe," said Desmond.
The bartender Joe turned away and said, "Yeah, you Were."

Mr. Stryker, Do You Really Want to Turn This Into Some Kind of a WAR!!!!!

The slightly older than middle aged man wears his sunglasses at the bus stop and squints towards the sun waiting for his number to come up.

The ground vibrates, he looks up, squints to make sure he has the right number, his greatest fear is getting on the wrong bus, he looks up, checks again, and he steps on.

He throws the words,"Stop 47," at the bus driver.

Why doesn't the bus have seat belts he wonders, as it rumbles and bumps over potholes and shakes on the boulevard.

He puts his face to the Plexiglas and looks for his stop, stop 47, the vibration of the bus always helps him darken reality and slide off to somewhere else, to a time where there were only two bus lines and the drivers were always the same.

He tries to fight his instincts by counting the various stops, 40, 42, but he loses somewhere around stop 44.

The slightly older than middle aged man wakes up at stop 58, his swollen eyes widen and he yells at the bus driver, "I told you I was stop 47." Through the rear view mirror the slightly older than middle aged man sees the bus driver rolling her eyes at him and shrugging her shoulders.

"People just don't give a damn anymore," he says just loud enough for her to hear.

"Maybe you should get a car old man," jokingly says a passenger across from him, a boy with big brown eyes wrapped in tall eyelashes, but with old man hands.

(Continued)

The driver stops half-way between 58 and 59, but only pulls over part of the way.

The slightly older than middle aged scowls and steps off the bus; he removes his sunglasses, and crosses the street, to catch the bus.

Back to the stop
that he missed.

"I know you weren't yourself when you did this, Hedy."

If your friend goes out of town and tells you to watch her cat, you should feed him coolant.
If she get's angry at you about her cat's death,
You know that she wasn't your friend anyway,
So that negative emotion brought about a positive action,
Ridding yourself of a person who was just using you while their cat was bored.
It's just a cat.
What kind of person cares more about their pet than their good friend that offered to not only watch their pet, but to pick up their newspaper and their mail?
Psychiatrists say killing squirrels and shooting birds is a sign of a demented mind.
Most psychiatrists are crazy.
My mother was a psychiatrist.
Killing your friend's pet, is a test, a good test.
People need tests.
The government tests you so you can have the privilege of shooting a gun.
The government tests you so you can have the privilege of killing people overseas
The government tests you so you can have the privilege of driving a tanker filled with poisonous gas
My college tested me so I could have the privilege of dropping $80,000 to learn how to sleep,
With my eyes open.
Friendship is a privilege not a right and it should be tested, constantly.
A dead pet isn't a lost,
It's a symbol,
A symbol of the strength or the weakness of your bond between you and another human being.
I fed my mother's poodle coolant when I was twelve, she got very upset about it,
That's how I knew
She wasn't my friend, just my dad's pet.
Daddy passed the test.
Go out and test a friend today.

Ben Sanderson told me,
"I thought I might move out to Las Vegas."

Don't worry
In LA no one dies
They just move away
Far
To somewhere like,
Riverside
or Las Vegas
Go into syndication
And make their kids
Watch their old show
Over and over
And over
Again

Liz Taylor Suite

things happen to everyone, some people are just better at
making them sound
sad-larkism

What Would Have Happened if Ms. Wandrous Hadn't Died

Glory is driving her car off Sunset Boulevard, into the ocean, in an attempt to downsize her life.

She is smoking her last Capri cigarette , so as she inhales, she is savoring every bit of the cloudy air.

Glory thinks she has finished her last bottle of pink oval pills.
Down the road she passes the place she spent four years doing her best perfection impressions: perfect virgin, perfect daughter, perfect girlfriend, and perfect mess.

Things seemed as if they moved along more interestingly before, but four years is four seconds when you drive by and flip your head back and perspective varies depending on the side of the building you pass by.

Glory has erased the idea of a detour on a destination to downsize, because detours just delay your destination and right now she has to get rid of this car.

Downshifting makes the metal go faster, as Glory pulls the stick into third, she goes down the blind curve that she got lost on once; she only traveled down it, because she thought it was a shortcut, it was not a shortcut, but it was faster.

When Sunset goes west it grips the hills of the wealth of the winners on the north and grips the flats of the dreams of the losers on the south and if you are not paying attention things happen.

Where Sunset intersects La Cienega is where Glory's happened, she crashed three years ago, a stupid guy hit her or maybe she was the stupid that hit him.

What Would Have Happened if Ms. Wandrous Hadn't Died (Continued)

The happen destroyed her vintage MG. Vintage is a subjective term. In LA even crap has a fancy name.

Driving the new car bought with her happening, she realizes that it needed to go, but at the beginning of her excursion somewhere around Wilton she had only planned on wrecking the car, but then as she was drove further west and passed LaBrea, near the Cat N Fiddle, she realized that a wreck would not make it go away.

Sunset Blvd is tricky to navigate when you go east and it turns into Caesar Chavez and it's even trickier to navigate when you go west and the signals disappear, but the middle seems easy, but that's where you always See people pulled over.

Speeding past Brentwood she throws out her wallet, her cell phone, her shirt, her trousers,
and even her shoes,
but she keeps her coat,
so she won't be completely indecent when she gets to the other side.

First impressions you know.

She hopes her coat does not get caught when she attempts to jump out of her car, but unbeknownst to Glory she'll never get to that point,
because Sunset Blvd doesn't end at the ocean,
it just turns into another street.

Benjamin Pinkerton Thinks I'm Cool

You are exotic not cute and that is a good thing, because it lasts longer.
We can last longer, because you are exotic not cute.
I can last longer, because you are exotic not cute.
I see in you, I can see inside.

You remind me of the past, you remind me of high school, you remind
of high school history class, you remind me of the dark, in high school
with my bedroom door locked and the radio turned loud and my mom
pounding on the door.

"Are you ok, what are you doing? Hey what are you doing, answer me!!"

And I teach high school, so it helps me to remember, so I can, I can see
you.

I can see the outside of you,
I can see the smell of you,
I can see the taste of you,
I can see the feel of you,

I can imagine all of you, as you stand and look at me from the left side of
the counter and you ask me to please pass the sugar for your scorching,
over-roasted, bitter Starbuck's coffee from some far off place in Latin
America, Asia, or Africa or some weird mix, because the manager forgot
to order enough, because he was hung over from the night before,

Coffee Bean's coffee isn't nearly as bitter, their coffees are a more com-
plicated, sophisticated blend.

So I will pass you the sugar, so that you can sweeten the coffee designed
for the masses with a less refined palate.

I am happy to help, I like helping, because you are exotic, not cute.

As a Hostess I Only Got Paid Extra for the Drinks

If you drop a lamp at a party in LA, just walk away.

Of course you feel bad, it is your friend, it's your friends stuff, but keep in mind it's just stuff,

And remember you two had that conversation the other day about the meaninglessness of stuff,
Buddhism and not being attached and all that kind of stuff, that people who got a lot stuff tend to be into.

Until their stuff, starts breaking.

"What was that?"
"What?"
"That."
"That's just the music, did you see the movie Sideways, it was actually quite good."

So if you drop a lamp at a LA party, just walk away.

I know in the Midwest, you don't do that,
I know on the East Coast, you don't do that,
I know in the South, you don't do that,

But out here in LA, in the land of the size two 50 year old housewife/consultant whose habit of prescription drugs makes her not get angry anymore at her cokehead 13 year old, who has a very special friendship with her husband's business associate, but at least the 13 year old isn't sleeping with her husband anymore, that was so much worse, what a little whore of a 13 year old,

We do that.

We walk away when we drop lamps,
We walk away if you drop,

(Continued)

We walk away from broken stuff.

Do you want to get sued?
Do you have unlimited income?
Are you a trust fund baby?
Are you perfect?

People who have business cards, will have to answer, no.

If you come from somewhere else,
Don't pick up a lamp, at a LA party,
Don't admit to breaking a lamp, at a LA party,
Don't admit to anything, at a LA party.

Maybe that guy is a producer or that gal is a director, maybe they have
had enough to drink to believe that you are perfect, beautiful, talented
and part of who they are, the they who are talented, beautiful, perfect.

You don't want to ruin that image of perfect, by being on your knees,
picking up pieces of glass.

Because that's where you will end up,
You won't be able to find the vacuum cleaner, because you'll be too
drunk, it will be dark, and if you do find it, you won't be able to turn it
on, you'll be sprawled out, looking up, trying to find a button, trying to
get it on, in the dark, by yourself,
while everyone else, is downstairs, having a good time and
laughing at you,
the person in the dark,
sprawled out
on the floor.

Don't pick up a broken lamp at a LA Party, because only out-of-towners
care about the broken pieces of glass on the bedroom floor.

Debbie Reynolds Was a Good Organizer

Dear Mrs X

I'm writing you this letter,
because your husband is my boyfriend,
I knew my boyfriend was married to You,
when I first started emailing him,
I looked it up on the internet
well, actually I knew for other reasons
I keep lying,
Sorry about that
I've heard recently that You sort of found out about us,
and that You cried,
that You cried a lot,
now I'm not going to try to explain anything,
there isn't much to explain
I don't think You should leave him
I know he's sorry
I'm sorry too, I'm actively trying to end this
I try to go out with other people, but I love my boyfriend,
who is your husband
he told me last night when he was in my bed
that he was real sorry and that he didn't mean to hurt You,
that he wants to stop hurting You
so I don't have any explanations,
I have some thoughts
I'll tell You what I thought
I thought he didn't like You
I thought maybe You were real mean,
but You seem not so mean and he seems to like You
he hasn't left You
he told me that he doesn't love me
he told me to not love him
I bet he's never told You that
You guys had a big wedding right

(Continued)

mainly what me and my boyfriend, who is also your husband,
mainly what we do is have sex
we watch porn and have sex
we have sex a lot
I do all the stuff that his wife, his wife being You, won't do
he tells me that I'm beautiful
that I have perfect breasts
I think he's just using me, because he's sad
but I'm kind of using him, because I'm sad too
we're both
sad people
I know You're unhappy about this situation,
but we're both sick, You are not,
so possibly You'll have mercy on us
I'm sincerely sorry, he's sorry too
he told me this morning on the phone, that he's sorry, that he didn't
mean to hurt You, I can't tell You that we're going to stop seeing each
other, because that's a lie and that would probably just hurt You more,
in the long-term
but I'll say this,
I'm sorry
every time I lie with him,
I'm sorry and I'm sure
he's sorry too
but don't leave him, because he loves You and he likes your cooking,
I could never make that dish he's always talking about or remember to
feed the cats or pay the bills,
he said You're a good organizer
so he needs You, I need You too, because if You left him
we would probably have to stop having sex as much,
we would probably stop having sex completely
And I'm pretty sure, eventually
someone would be writing me a letter similar to this one
and that would kill me

Debbie Reynolds Was a Good Organizer
(Continued)

I'm sick You know
You're a strong woman,
You can handle this kind of thing
I'm weak, so I couldn't
So in closing,
I would like to offer You my deepest apologies,
I thought You were mean,
but You're not

Thursday/Friday/Saturday

I was standing at a party and I was smoking and I was flirting with a
man that I shouldn't have been flirting and wearing a dress I paid too
much for that was cut too low and I didn't have a bra on and I was being
generally rude and unpleasant and I sneered at the person holding the
hor d'oeuvre trays and not because she did anything, but because she
was there and then this person came up to me and started talking about
Bernie and how we should all really vote for blah, blah, blah, blah, blah,
blah and then I excused myself to the open bar, because I don't care
--and I was there to have a good time and it's not like I vote anyway,
not because of some political reason, but because I don't care and I don't
want to talk to people who still care at least not at a party, because I was
drunk and I was focused on the guy I was flirting with earlier and I was
thinking if I should have sex with him, but then because I'm Catholic I
started feeling a little guilty about sneering at the lady holding the hor
d'oeuvre tray, so I went back up to her and I told her that I liked her
hair, even though I didn't--- because I thought that would be the nice
Catholic thing to do even though I hadn't been to Mass since I graduated
from Mount St Mary's-- and she sort of just stared at me like I was an
asshole.

I am not an asshole!

And then I started thinking wow it's been 15 years since I graduated
from college and the only thing that has changed about me is that I have
more expensive clothes and hang out in better bars and that reflection
lasted for about 45 seconds because that guy came up to me again and
he was talking about how he was writer and listing all the magazines
he had written for and I thought why is he giving me his resume, it's
11:50 p.m. and this isn't a job interview and it's not like this can lead to
anything beyond really horrible regrettable sex, so then I decided to go
to the bathroom and do some coke, which is really 1985ish, but I love the
80s, especially the music, but then in the bathroom blood started gush-
ing out of my nose and I was wondering is this some kind of sign from
god and I said it aloud and then god responded:

Thursday/Friday/Saturday

(Continued)

"It's a sign that you're using too many drugs."

But when I looked behind me it wasn't God, it was a woman with the best bob I'd ever seen. I always felt if I had straight hair that I would have a bob, but I don't so I won't so I went back out to the party and the guy was still there and he started talking about how he was from New York and about his family and then he asked if I wanted a drink and I was like of course I want a drink and I told him to get me a double and he said SURE and so I waited and he came back and handed me the drink, a drink I quickly threw down my throat and then he asked me if I wanted to get food and I said, "if it is at your house."

Then there was a pause and he said: "OK."

The next morning and I drove home and went to sleep and woke up at 5 p.m. and then a few hours later I was standing at a party and I was smoking and I was flirting with a man that I shouldn't have been flirting and wearing a dress I paid too much for that was cut too low.

Mr. Humbert, Democrat, Retired Third Grade Teacher, and Open Mike Host

Hello, how are you?

Are you going to read, I am assuming that you are, since you just signed the sign-in sheet, make sure to sign up for our newsletter.

We sometimes have younger members at our readings.

Do any of your poems have questionable content, the kind of content that arouse younger members.

How did you hear about us, where are you from?

We don't like dirty stuff Here, the other week we had this gentleman and he started reading and his poem had questionable, content and we stopped him, I stopped him, I said, "No you can't do that, you can't do that Here."

Your poems aren't like that, are they, they aren't, you know, dirty?

I've got children, a seven year old, an eight year old, and a thirteen year old, all boys, I wish my wife had a little girl, little girls are so pretty, I've got a neighbor that has a little girl
and she always has a little bit of dirt on her face,
what a dirty little girl,
so cursing it's ok, but you have to be able to read your audience,
some people can't read their audience,
you have to be able to See what you can or can not say.

I have some poems and they have some curse words in them, because I'm not conservative,
but they aren't dirty.

Mr. Humbert, Democrat, Retired Third Grade Teacher, and Open Mike Host   (Continued)

You aren't dirty, you aren't a dirty girl are you,
because if you are we'll stop you, I'll go on stage and I'll pull you off, I'll
drag you off, you know this is a family establishment, this is a place where
people take their families, so we expect you to respect that,

You aren't the kind of person who likes being drugged and restrained?

Is that one of your poems that you are editing?
Again how did you say that you found out about us, oh?

So you came from LA, what part of LA,

you know I used to teach at Gompers,
I was teaching there during the riots,
that was pretty horrible,
is that near Hollywood?

You aren't dirty are you, you aren't a dirty girl, we promote a family
atmosphere, family values, my wife, she's a teacher, she's a poet too, we
have been married for 17 years, so what is it that you do besides poetry,
you look sort of like a dancer, dancers are pretty flexible,
are you a dancer who writes dirty poems?

So have you read other places around here, are you Well-Known?

That guy who read here the other week, he was talking about some
woman rimming him, that's not the type of stuff you do, because this is a
public place, a family place, a Christian place, I mean we aren't all
Republican, I view myself as a fiscally conservative,
socially conscious liberal,
I hate Bush.

(Continued)

Bush is bad.
Bush is evil.
Bush is dirty.

You don't talk about stuff like bukkake and frottage and slings and
spankings and fisting and analingous and flagellation and harnesses
and submission and voyeurism and candy makers and daisy chains and
urolagnia and doing blumpkins and bird-watching and helping ladies
and gentlemen earn their redwings, that's not the type of stuff you talk
about, is it,
because we don't like that stuff around
Here.

So are you or are you not a dirty girl?

Dorothy Dandrige Suite

the right outfit, can make just about anyone -- seem
interesting.-larkism

The Doll's Hour or the Truth About Barbie

Barbie and Ken got divorced and Barbie moved in with Raggedy Ann
and they became partners.

Ken was happy the charade was over,
I'm sure you all read about the divorce in the papers.

Her agent, Bob Mattel, was a little worried about her popularity.

What if the public found out that Barbie was living with a cloth doll?

The courts removed Skipper,
Barbie's little sister from the Dream House,
because according to them a plastic doll and a cloth doll being together
is considered an unnatural
and an inappropriate environment to raise a plastic child in,
but Raggedy Ann's brother Andy is an excellent attorney,
Dartmouth.

It is a little awkward at times,
because Raggedy Ann doesn't exactly fit in the Dream House,
but Barbie and Ann seem very happy.

Sometimes Barbie has a hard time walking for long periods,
because of her oversize breast and her tiny feet that are a little mal-
formed, because of a lifelong addiction to high heels,

But since Ann has a comfy front pocket,
Barbie often hitches a ride inside it,
And that's something that she could never do with Ken.

Barbie and Ken are still really good friends.

Ken is living with He-Man in a condo in WeHo.

No I can't Spare a Dime you Evil Human
(a proposal in action)

The reason why tofu tastes so good is because it's made out of new born babies.

Soybean, soylent green, it's people you get it.

Tofu is little baby people.

It's dead baby meat killed fresh from their mother's womb,
well the betters tofu is,
the kind you get at Real Food Daily in Santa Monica;
the frozen type,
well they are a little older,
but still pretty young,
under four.

People are evil and bad, so eating a person isn't really that disgusting,
not disgusting like an alive person doing annoying things,
like cutting you off on the freeway
or asking for change when you are trying to get a drink at the Golden Golpher.

Eating a chicken or a lamb or a cow or even an altoid, yuck that's just gross.

But baby people,
they aren't real,
they don't think or feel,
yeah chickens don't think either,
but chickens aren't evil,
like little baby people are.
not fetuses,
but little baby people, the ones in orphanages,
yeah orphanages they still exist,

(Continued)

but now they are given euphemisms, like
Amy's Kitchen or Fantastic
and
Trader Joe's run them.

The people who don't have families and aren't going to ever get foster
parents
are given to Trader Joe's
or subsidiaries of Trader Joe's
and are ground up to make tofu,
so we can enjoy
soy burgers.

At first I found it kind of disturbing,
because people meat is still meat,
but then I realized
being vegetarian isn't about people
it's about saving nonhuman animals.

The only good kind of animal
is a non-human one,
so then I felt much better about it.

Dead baby meat,

yummy.

#DTLA is not Racist!

The black guy
is masturbating on Sixth again
These homeless people are getting ridiculous
There is this program up north,
where they nicely ship them away for work programs
It is really nice
I don't know if happy adverbs can make an internment camp sound OK
Molina just cares about the Latinos
Molina hates white people
She doesn't have a bike
She didn't go to the bike meeting
We need more cops
We need more security
Another black guy
masturbating
I have a picture, I got up at at 4 am and I caught him
My dog needs a place to run
Can we make that park private?
We are bringing back Broadway
Those businesses weren't real
You know what we mean
I find your accusation that I am racist offensive
Here we go again with the race card, you people and the race card
My name is James T Butts and I am Black and I am here to let you know
that Bob isn't
racist
That black homeless guy is out of control
No one was even talking about race
Obama is the best president ever
This time it's an Asian guy masturbating on Seventh
Did not know they could be homeless?
I thought that was a black thing
What? I am not being offensive just honest
I went out with an Asian lady once

(Continued)

She was real Americanized and talked too much
I had to break up with her
I am not racist, the Irish were the first slaves I am not Irish, but I could
be
There you go again with the race card
Race is relevant here
your accusations of racism
are why you people are masturbating
all over this place
And I voted for Obama,
I told you that.

Jane Fonda Doesn't Just Exercise

Today I'm taking off my Che t-shirt and putting on a white gown, because I'm getting married to a great guy.

A spectacularly, great guy.

On our honeymoon we are going to Paris.

I met him at this rally protesting the proliferation of cigarette butts off the shores of Lough Derravaragh,
that's in Ireland,
in case you don't know,
that was patronizing of me wasn't it, so sorry, I do that all the time,
because I'm brilliant, I hope that is ok with you, some people don't like me, jealous of my brilliance.

Do you know my dress is couture, can you believe it, I feel guilty, but it's my special day.

I'm not a conventional person, I'm bisexual, I'm an activist, I'm a support-er of oppressed peoples, I'm a far leftist, and I'm a feminist.

When I was in college I had a girlfriend, but we broke up after I graduated, because I thought that kind of a lifestyle wasn't for me, and I like guys, but you know you have to experience everything, that's why I once went out with this guy who was a foreign exchange student from the Middle East, now when I go to rallies protesting the war it gives me an edge on the other protesters in regards to perspective.

There's going to be an open bar.

I'm not a conventional person, I have done so many things, and even what I look like, I mean I can't even begin to count the number of colors I have had my hair dyed and I have over 10 body piercings, I know to you right now I look almost totally normal, but I'm working as a

(Continued)

fundraiser in Century City and to help people sometimes you have to conform to help them a little more.

I had to book 13 months in advance to get this church.

The great guy I'm marrying he's one of our top donors, so that means he cares a lot, well maybe I didn't meet him at a rally, maybe it was more of a dinner or maybe it was after the dinner at the Mountain Bar, but it was for an important cause,
it was about the proliferation of cigarette butts off the shores of Lough Derravaragh, that's in Ireland,
in case you don't know.

He told me the night we met, you can help more from the inside.

You can fix the problem by becoming the problem and through nice dinners you might be able to convince them to be more empathetic.

We are going to be in an excellent school district, but I'm thinking, private school.

I'm going to miss my place though, but not so much, last week this couple moved next door with a kid, I mean come on these are one bedrooms and besides he's got a place in Newport Beach and it's much bigger than mine, so that's why I'm leaving my pad with the people, but nothing is going to change.

Everyone can wear their hair the way they want, this isn't a traditional wedding, I have a reggae band.

Yeah I'm going to be the same person,
because I won't be changing my last name,
because as long as you don't change your last name. the other stuff doesn't matter so much.

Random Violence

My great-great grandfather came to Los Angeles in 1890 after taking the
opportunity of slitting his father's throat
in an act of random violence
in New Orleans

His father --my great-great-great-grandfather had the biggest and most
luxurious home in the Garden District in New Orleans.

Some people called it a plantation.

America has always been a violent country

And Los Angeles

Has always been

a violent town.

It exists owing to murder and lies, but murders and lies opens the door for
opportunities for random violence.

In 1900 my great-great grandfather opened a bar and out of it he sold as he
called it-- opportunities.

Some people called him a loanshark.
Some people said my great-great grandfather was a violent man.

My great-grandfather continued running the bar and the business of opportunities and then gave it to my grandfather.

My grandfather used these opportunities to send my mother to UCLA
and she became the first legitimate member of the Molyneux family, but I
always liked my grandfather.

(Continued)

I would hang out with him in the bar, help him clean his gun and help him balance his books.

One day we were walking up Central Avenue.

And a man walked up to us and attempted to grasp his opportunity. He told my grandfather that he wanted his money.

He seemed to have a gun in his pocket.

My grandfather gave him an opportunity and asked him if he was sure and did the young man know who he was and did the young man see he was with his favorite granddaughter the young man said,
"Give me your fucking money old man."

My grandfather took out his silver gun, a gun I had pointed at my sister's head a week prior in a game of cops and robbers,
and shot him in the arm.

The young man said with disbelief, "You shot me."

And my grandfather said, "You tried to rob me and you better run, before I make it so you can't run anymore."

The young man ran away. I guess he didn't have a gun and my grandfather looked at me and said, "Beak, what did you learn." He called me Beak because my name was Lark which is a bird and birds have beaks and I talk a lot.

I said, "That if you walk outside that people will try to rob you,"
And he said, "No, that's not the lesson. The lesson is, if you try to rob people, you will get shot."

Random Violence

(Continued)

At the bar the following week while drinking the root beer float my grandfather made me on Fridays after school
a murder in South Central was reported on the television.

They flashed a picture of a young man who was laid out on the sidewalk
with yellow tape surrounding his body filled with bloody holes.

The reporter said, "In a case of random violence in South Central LA a
young man was killed."

I looked over at my grandfather from the bar stool and he smiled and
asked me did I like my treat and I smiled back and nodded my head yes.

And that's the day I learned that you don't pull a gun on a gangster unless
you plan on killing him
and there is no such thing as
random violence.

Napoleon Ate Snowball and Nobody Noticed

SUVs are massive and they always try to squeeze into a spot which is
perfect for my latest hybrid.

They squeeze into lanes, squeeze into spots, squeeze past yellow lights.

Squeezing into where they do not belong, like a wide ass squeezing into
pair of jeans which used to look good,
but now
not quite right,
not now,
not anymore,
but the darkness covers up the awkward bulges, so the ass just keeps
wearing them.

Things that squeeze never signal, they just get over,
it's not that I would let them over if they did signal,
but they don't signal,
they just squeeze their way in,
squeezing their way into my space.

If I'm on a road and on my way to Whole Foods, I don't understand
why I have to wait for a SUV with a mom and her kids,
what are they doing, where are they going,
what I have to do is important,
in addition to my 1930 Triumph I have the latest hybrid that emits water
vapors, which shows that I care,
and what I have to do is
important.

I don't have any kids,
because I don't want to populate this overpopulated planet with more
things that people don't care about,
I don't want to have to focus on anything, but working on me being a
better person, so I can help the most people possible,

Napoleon Ate Snowball and Nobody Noticed
(Continued)

when I have some energy left, I need to focus so I can concentrate on my
vegetarian diet, my free random oppressed person causes,
and my greater understanding for the world around
me.

People who have children, they are selfish and unthinking,
there are plenty of children in countries that we are supposed to be happy
that we don't live in,
that's children we can adopt,
and those kids, they are grateful,
my friend gave money to an agency that procured him a beautiful little girl
and he is very, very, very happy.

I don't celebrate holidays, because they aren't real,
just devices to market cards.

I hate my mother.

SUVs, packed full of kids, taking over our roads,
squeezing into where they don't belong, taking spaces that belong to us,
the good people who drive little cars like the VW convertible, my weekend
car, that run on little amounts of gas
and little amounts of electricity.

Who are these people,
who are these people who don't understand,
who don't care,
how can they be so selfish,
so intolerant,
so greedy
of our limited space.

This is MY space.

Those wicked selfish people!!!

Acknowledgments/About the Author

This book was written with the help of my many experiences growing up in Los Angeles. I was born in Los Angeles in the neighborhood now known as Koreatown. Most of my 20s were spent in Los Feliz and Silver Lake. Many of my friends from the late 90s and Roaring Aughts have passed on owing to their excesses. I would list their names, but out of respect for their families I will not. My household was pleasant. My mother and father are good people. They are why I wrote this book, because the good people deserve to have vindication. I understand all of the things my parents taught me, though I may not show it in a literal fashion.

I would like to thank my dear friend Mark who taught me many things on a swing in San Pedro. I would also like to thank Lewis MacAdams, who though a Texan is still L.A. cool.

Dr. Charles Sontag IV saved me from certain death in December of 2015. I thank him the most for allowing me to write another day. Finally, I would like to thank my editor Paul Portuges and Word Palace Press, my publisher.

Other Books from Word Palace Press

How Strange it is to Be Anything at All by Joe Riley

On Tibetan Buddhism, Mantras and Drugs by Allen Ginsberg

Instructions for the Living by Mariko Nagai

Border Songs by Sam Hamill

Frets and Struts by Barry Spacks

Under Such Brilliance by Kevin Sullivan

Beauty Like a Rope by Leslie St. John

Wayfaring Stranger by Richard Tillinghast

Who on Earth by Michael Hannon

Celtic Light by Lee Perron

Tilting Point by Peter Dale Scott

Life by Jack Foley

Imaginary Burden by Michael Hannon

A Poem of Miracles by Jerome Rothenberg

How One Loses Notes and Sounds by Teresa Mei Chuc

The Village Sonnets by Michael Lally

Women Under the Influence by Michael C Ford

The Muse Turns Her Back by Michael Hannon

Upcoming Titles

Sister Madeline by Joe Riley

The Human Field by Tran Quang Quy
(Translated by Nguyen Phan Que Mai & Jennifer Fossenbell)

Pina Bausch by Werner Lambersy (Translated by Jack Hirschman)

CPSIA information can be obtained
at www.ICGtesting.com
Printed in the USA
LVHW092330290921
699095LV00010B/98

9 780975 465332